Round Lake

Round Lake

Grace Bonner

Four Way Books
Tribeca

for my mother and sister

Please direct all inquiries to:
Editorial Office
Four Way Books
POB 535, Village Station
New York, NY 10014
www.fourwaybooks.com

LLibrary of Congress Cataloging-in-Publication Data

Names: Bonner, Grace.
Title: Round lake / Grace Bonner.
Description: New York, NY : Four Way Books, 2016.
Identifiers: LCCN 2016007104 | ISBN 9781935536741 (pbk. : alk. paper)
Classification: LCC PS3602.O657425 A6 2016 | DDC 811/.6--dc23
LC record available at https://lccn.loc.gov/2016007104

This book is manufactured in the United States of America and printed on acid-free paper.

Four Way Books is a not-for-profit literary press. We are grateful for the assistance
we receive from individual donors, public arts agencies, and private foundations.

This publication is made possible with public funds from the New York State Council on the Arts,
a state agency

and from the Jerome Foundation.

[clmp]

We are a proud member of the Community of Literary Magazines and Presses.

Distributed by University Press of New England
One Court Street, Lebanon, NH 03766

CONTENTS

THREE

A sister is an Old World sparrow placed in a satin shoe.

—Lucie Brock-Broido, "Dove, Interrupted"

And the dear ordinary had healed as seamlessly as an image on water.

—Marilynne Robinson, *Housekeeping*

INCANTATION

My sister didn't   want to live   a serpent   in her heart

a serpent   who couldn't   be charmed   when she fell

it was deliberate   I tried   to make   her stay

we sat around   the kitchen table   noon darkening   she was gone

I went to Greece   to see   mermaid mosaics   and heard

my sister lost   her mind   in jail   fragmented angels

bear her up   what happened   killed our mother   left a serpent

in my heart   her hissing hair   and steady gaze   she had a gun

she disappeared   protect me mother   heart a serpent   must be charmed

ONE

Round Lake, NY

(1)

I remember waking
    in bluer depths,

my moon-mouth
    gulping air,

hungry for
    no one.

SHIP GLIMPSED FROM THE WIDOW'S WALK

I telescope you out to the farsighted wrong
end of the instrument

till you're a speck of microscopic trouble.
To find you here, all found out,

is no bad miracle: I haven't missed a day
of lookout in thirty years.

Your prow quivers like the sea
lions, who heave their flesh

to sunnier rocks. A white ship on the horizon
is worth ten in battle.

Now pack up your religions. It's time
to set the table.

LANDSCAPE WITH COLOSSAL KOUROS

Samos lay me down to sleep,
thirty brown-stained fish in a yawning cove.
Weary of waves, urchins, and cigarette butts,
the abandoned lighthouse couldn't care less
if we stay or go. Sirocco settles the matter
for a ferry caught in horseshoe harbor.
Hailstones pummel Hera's temple;
wind plays shepherd huts like dropped stone flutes.
Stranded, I don't know whether to curse
or thank the Furies—punishers of perjurers—
for another night in the arms of a man
who cannot love me.
Sculptors of colossal Kouroi inscribed
not only a name in the statue's thigh
but for whom he was made. Vainly, I scan
my lover's body for a monogram.

PLAYING BACH

I'm building up
       the silent bones
with a distracting love
       of music.

Words scale
       and fall in a
similar way,
       like hands letting

one field lie
       fallow to favor
another. You were gone
       like a paper lantern

in a ceremony
       for Daimonji.
Hands place thousands
       of lights in the river,

one by one. They form
       a thin, glowing snake
on water, bobbing
       a subtle "S" shape.

The ceremony
    seems miraculous.
How can it be,
    I wonder, the river

isn't crowded?
    What about
the other candles?
    In a moment,

I understand. A monk
    on the other side
plucks the ones
    drifting his way,

and covers them.
    He arranges the snuffed
lanterns on the bank
    in neat, endless rows.

We should be careful
    of each other; yes.
God is more meticulous
    than kind.

Poem for Jesus's Son

his body
a ladder
to the sky

he rains
sweet whiskey
and cigarettes

nobody
I mutter
at the clouds

nobody
rolls such
sweet thunder

Sunken Table

The last time I saw
white blossoms, I put

one petal
on my tongue,
stuck it

to the roof
of my mouth,
and pushed

my stocking foot up
the leg of your jeans.

But now,
when I kiss
your hand,

and your warm,
dry fingers
fill me,

and your ring
leaves fitful
traces,

this snow is dancing
on a lake

where everybody
drowns.

Dreamway

Every highway has a thousand ghosts,
and every ghost a thousand exits.

We line up for the Dreamway,
the nation's first limited-access

divided highway. With a ciggy
in one hand, the other spinning

Fortune's wheel, my sister's good
at getting lost. Not her dark hair dripping

from a late-morning shower;
not even the weight of her acoustic

can keep trash bags of clothes—
criminally loved—

from flying out the back.
Later, pink cords, rhinestone belt.

Hey you: see those dotted lines?
Or the barred ones, at least?

They indicate *most* distinctly
how not to drive like an asshole-ghost.

ELEGY

You stop the car, lie down in the road
for a meteor shower. Like Thetis, I lift you
by the heels, heave your dead weight
to the shoulder. I couldn't save you.
But we did cross the country one July,
sweltering in your Honda, special-ordered
sans A/C to save the Earth. We laughed
at God's unsubtle billboard: *You think*
it's hot here? You gripped the wheel,
shifted gears as if loading ammunition.
We shared a yen for the coast,
found North Carolina heaven almost.
Though the mountains are safer than home,
your absence is no relief, not like you'd hoped.

QUARREL IN SUMMER

A lamb crossed her face when she sensed the storm.
Then I realized it was not one,

but many lambs moving in the same direction
over untended fields. Hooves wrested

her features to grass. So I curled on the forehead
and slept under rain-

blackened trees. I was fitted for this, to exist
in the liable interstices

between heartbeats. Between fence posts,
hot mess of juniper. To stand before

a soul dividing—to outlive her.

GRAVITY AND GRACE

My sister says to a camera:
You have no idea the pain
I'm in right now.

She looks fine, physically.
Looks great, in fact.
I have heard her mistake a car service operator

for a God who cares.
Would someone please come,
would someone please come to deliver me—

I have placed the phone in its cradle
and put her drunk to bed.
She wrote a letter about recovery:

We just got back from taking Roxie
on a long walk by the beach and I feel
really good. The exercise and fresh air

helped, despite the cold and fog
(I accidentally typed "god").
The night after you left,

I dreamed about ghosts. I know this
might sound stupid, but was the Midwest
once covered with trees, like Pennsylvania,

and when people cut them down,
they just stopped growing?

Was good or fog your accidental god?
Where were *we* while our ghosts lived it up?
I've seen that English bulldog of yours hunt fog

for pinecones. She carries them one by one,
round and rough in her muzzle; drops them
at our feet, comes running back

on sand and shell *to deliver me.*
Her gravity is grace, and as gratuitous.
An accidental god topples me faster

than the world to come. Sister,
the tall-grass prairies are long gone.

LUCY

You strip me of my faith,
and leave me with Saint Lucy's eyes.

Once, on an island
near where I lived,

I saw you painted white
in a moat of thorns.

I remember swimming, then
scalding my hand.

TWO

Round Lake, NY

(2)

After loss, the heart
      tethers, like a kayak,

to the nearest, fixed body.
      It will cancel pleasure,

say the rain and mice
      that gnaw through my house.

Your Last Drive

Here by the highway you returned,
and flicked cigarette ashes, the only stars
bristling your sky.

And on your left, you blessed the girls
born in the Middle West, half-hidden
behind cash registers.

You shut a wasp-wing door,
took a footbridge to a border town
to flood your veins.

Your eyebrows that were never plucked,
the cowlick rising from a widow's peak,
your beautiful body unmarked by any tattoo—

you hid from me, and everyone. So what?
Toyota made half a million models
of your pickup,

and every other one leaves trails
of Arcade Fire.
You are past love, care, addiction, blame.

St. Just

Look how fast the clouds are moving
but down here there isn't any wind.

Loves-lies-bleeding bows its heads
in tassels up the cliff-side.

Smallest breath
floods a chambered cairn:

air pushes down the fields,
and the rocks are said to moan.

The sound requires compression
and an opening—

COVE

Undertow reminds: you've changed,
you haven't. Unwholesome, to act

so young. Waves say death comes
next, the only thing that will reduce you

to order. They say the world is mine,
let your calm enter my hands.

Come on, no pleasure is mine
except your calm, fast in my hands.

Lady with an Ermine

Despite one querulous, raised paw,
the ermine is being held. I am not.
Unseemly, it claws

the selvage of her sleeve.
It is a sin against nature
to send via the ear

those things that should be sent
via the eye, the painter wrote.
Hearing can deceive more readily

than sight, as tortuous sound
waves hurtle the dark
to make a far-off siren

overtake your breathing
next to me. But the lady
is faithful in her lift of hand

to ermine's shoulder blade,
whose white, mutable fur
is winter.

LETTER TO A GOWANUS NOVICE

No matter my want, canal prince, you rock,
plead with, sigh and seek to bend
o'er too many who are not your friends.
That you may rise in me again, forsake
all hussies; you know I cannot share you.
My heart, like the G train, catalectic
and marked by kitten heels, swerves at Smith
and Ninth. Yet, why not believe your body,
bruis'd, love-scratched, fell from a tree?
Shatter your rosy speeches, canal prince.
Let me alone, or let me be the only one to fix
your Catherine window in Gowanus.

WILL NOT BE QUIET

Come with me to the mountains, you fool.
Stop trying to tell me we're not meant,
the bandage over your forearm my sorrow can't heal.
You'd rather bear my anatomy
than say you're sorry, but lust doesn't happen
when you travel. It's only the alarm
of everyday doorbells, coattails,
makes you want to undress.
That bruise-colored spill of berries down the crag
when you speak will not be quiet.
Your chalice shows you mirrored,
upside down as hell looks from heaven.
What you want is a moonlit pool.
What you need is to lay me down
in a moonlit pool, rocked by wind.

ON THE ORIGINS OF LANGUAGE

Hello, Old Pleistoscene!
Hi, Holocene & big-headed infants.

What's shakin', Great Migration?
I think we left because we didn't

like our parents. Heigh-ho! The Tower
of Babel was a mystery ceremony

with Shaman Mitochondrial Eve
domesticating fire. Hello, stone knife.

Hey hey hey adaptation, needles, fishing poles. . .
"Hello, what-can-I-love-you-with?"

Siri, dear, would you please
refill Turkana Basin with precipitation,

and my body with a similar joy
the next time I go to bed with a man?

Make the life we bring back good,
and that which we create

communicate that we're still apes
with no idea of what we need.

Faerie Child

Lately,
I have glimpsed
a fabulous sea quince

in sequins;
sometimes two
or three sea quinces

in sequence;
and paid
no consequence.

The August in You

is vine-broken wood

is evidence

is beginning to sound

like a raindrop

had me barefoot, searching

for cats huddled

in the shed

is awareness

of blue hydrangea

where the walls are

weak, is awareness

of blue glass beads

Unnerving Groundcover

Chrysanthemum poison must be extracted
       before the petals are steeped for tea.
And so our love is like surgery:
       you pluck aphids from my brain, expect
a blossoming return.
       There are libraries and hospitals
for your recurrent disappointments.

       Lamb's ears may bandage wounds.
Don't come back, motherwort.
       You should know by now my garden is
traditionally English.
       A tattered velvet jacket left behind
from someone's recent tantrum in the hawthorns.
       We'll go to seed in sun-soaked sleeves,
cufflinks vain as cattails.

On a Boeing 757

I'm writing in the dark to protect myself.
In front of me, a stranger
has the back of your head.
He could be watching
Gilda on the silent monitor;
I can't be sure but can be
of other things: how pleasing,
the prospect of seeing you.
Man with the back of your head
glances quickly left, then back down.
Gray temples, the flash of glasses—
I think we never understood each other,
in winter, speeding to Mass,
you smoking with the windows sealed—
his hair, like yours, is
secretly wavy, beneath that tonic.
Was it the tumor or a change of mind
when you mailed me that Polaroid
of a willow planted years before?
Technicolor-blue sky, the old rain gutter
jarred the composition—
a child might've taken better.

But the photo is a window to the breaking
through of you to me.
You have lifted me into the air—

Anemone

Out of the blackest
violet spot,
a friend appears
in the part
most painted-over,
slim flags calling
no truce.

SPECTACULAR CREPUSCULAR

Green-spiked leaves
serrate the crown vetch
swarm: touch them,

smooth as teeth.
Who hid you here,
poured sleep across

your lips—crushed
violets, oleander—
for you to wake alone,

garlanded, spectacular?
What besides heat
makes you eternal?

We count the same
tribe of deer, unseen
in daylight. Somewhere,

a spider's spinneret
terminates its thread.

Marksman, Flourishing

You're in hands of perpetual care,

    but I'm still here, just shy

of meeting the Marksman halfway.

    Listen: a wrong note in the middle

of things; a warm, January heart.

    There's no modesty anywhere anymore.

You've slipped through how many

    hands of care, spent weeks traveling

the unspeakable, little rowboat

    harnessed to a bristling hereafter.

A buckle fastens. Rope frays; we fashion

    new tools for the flourishing Marksman.

Effortless Traveler

when you blinked against the sun just now,
on your train home, where you won't be

for a thousand years, the closing of your lids
moved cathedrals down your face.

THREE

Round Lake, NY

(3)

Each day
    comes up

for breath,
    breaks

like a hymen,
    fills me

with wonder.
    Recovery is

these tiger lilies,
    voice of

an old friend.
    I'm OK, I

think. I think
    I'm OK.

LETTER TO MY SISTER

On the mountain where I live, rehearsal
for the dog, cock, and donkey chorus starts
each morning before dawn. Do you know
what wakes them? Yesterday, I climbed
a mountain to the monastery, the main one
above town. The oldest olive tree has been there
two thousand years. I wish you could see
its massive roots break the stone courtyard.
When I touched the olive—
my hands were bleeding from the climb—
I saw an image of your face and knew
it had seen you, too. We danced a votive for you.
This is the closest we've been.

NAOUSSA

Doves fly,
trouble a sky
whiter than sun.

Stones once
steep Naoussa cliffs
fit in the palm.

Barefoot,
my lady comes
downrushing.

Feathers
over shut eyes
rain pale light.

Waves glance
vertiginously
where she went.

Song Traversing a Tenebrous World

Children pretend to be planes, arms raised,
laughing until they crash into one another
in the narrow, whitewashed streets.

It's Great Friday in Greece. People mourn
as though a villager has died.
Was it you, Sister?

From behind strands of salt-hardened hair,
she stares to the back of beyond.
I feel her eyes, hungry to be gone.

I have passed her along the coast,
her retinue of Coors Light
and a hundred thousand unrecorded songs.

Each time she appears, I'm sure will be
the last, that next time she'll turn up
in seine nets, newly mended after months

of plunder. *Be a genius at something else*

I tell her, when I don't want to kill her.

Or: *I love the way you play guitar.*

If I find her in the sun

with her back against a tree, eyes closed,

bottles away, she's beatific.

Mother Last June

I watch her gardening.
See how her hands mix with soil.

See how she crouches down,
yanks weeds up by the roots.

Is it important: early evening?
Is it important: a note, taped to glass?

I have circled our yard, calling her name.
And the stream paces like a lion caged near fire.

GREENPOINT

I'm stirring a porcini sauce that makes me miss you,
smoking pot, with the phone off, I can pretend

you might've called, when I become aware of something
outside the kitchen window: it's a presence

watching my every stir. At first, I can't see, but feel it
dreaming me back to normal.

I'm just relaxing after work, making dinner.
You'll be home soon. The sense is overwhelming

when I slide the window open. A little wasp wanders in—
Damn Nature!— dances by the stove,

intoxicated by tomato bed.
Kali whirls a skirt of arms;

Jesus takes cover under Japanese tea roses.
I thought you couldn't get any smaller—

help me become older, Mother.

BAT BABY

She invades the mountain house.
Wind of her webby wingspan snuffs
the most courageous lamps.
I'm caught in her anxious figure.
Artemidorus translates in his *Oneirocritica:*
if a woman is dreaming, the man she loves
prefers art. Bad marriage. If the dreamer
is a man: success, pomegranates.
You're awake, my lover says, *make a spoon.*
Baby won't clear the sill of my mind,
and I doubt she ever will.
She dives above a hall of cypress
planted long ago by rich Venetians.

House of Beth

All hearts beat, and some break,
in pelvic parentheses.
After my mother died, I decided not to
have my own child.
Then I dreamed I changed my mind.
When asked why I was born,
she said, *I wanted to see
what you would look like.*
Her last note was addressed
to the ones she loved.
The qualifier seems strangely limited.
What about the ones she'd not yet met
but would have loved?
The future ones—are they included, implicitly?
The missive is precise and contains
an em-dash, a semicolon,
and devastating parentheses.
My computer says "House of Beth"
already exists. It asks if I want
to cancel; replacing overwrites it.
To grieving friends and wild children
I will never know—love,
love must be bearable.

GIRL WITH DOVES

Sculptor shatters
marble, makes

her millennia
contrapposto.

Her peplos stays
unbelted.

Hard lips press
a dainty beak,

forever captive.

CROOK AND CRADLE

Armistice Day, 2003

Out of body

    armor, lightweight

maneuverable riot

    helmet, yoke/collar;

out of throat/groin

    cover; out of

survivability; out of

    modified interceptor;

out of tailored-

    to-specific threats;

out of exceeding

    vests; out of full

spectrum; out of

    hydration system

compatibles; out of beast

    ballistics; out of grain

fragmentation; out of middle

    west; out of sea

bottom; out of quicksilver

caress; out of rings,

glasses, superannuated

grandfather pocket watches;

out of glinting heat;

out of the crook

of a hill's dark arms,

boys and girls are

cradled as they fall.

Out of metal light;

out of bloody mess;

out of a hill's

black chest; out of red

afterimages;

out of the lightest,

most protective system

ever; out of sight—

FALASSARNA

Themis, blindfolded
with drawn sword

dances on the backs of
immortal horses,

parrying all-out-war.
My sister calls me to arms.

I take dead stars
from policemen's uniforms

and place them in a jar
in Falassarna,

hatching butterflies
in Falassarna.

ANXIETY

Williamsburg, Brooklyn

Light's long hand cups
the patinated dome.

Birds know what is to come
and this and this.

How is it, after all I've tried,
read, prayed to,

I still fear my dark moods.
I hold my own hand

to cross the street
and calm myself

by the Russian cathedral
in late December.

Five green cupolas
twirl an hour

I've seen before
and this and this—

the certainty of light's
long hand.

MOTHLIGHT

What's left of you
arrives in morning
sun streaming.

I hold a sack-flour
baby's weight over
my heart.

Unlike a real child's
head in my arms,
you can't feel me.

I carry you west
to New Mexico
in August.

Milk-colored clouds
over Highway Four
desert us.

Wind picks up,
constellating sand.

Your new room has
walls of stars.

Thin Place

you are thin   you are light   I hold you

up to   the light   pin me

to the earth   again my loves   you are

thin   you are light   I hold

my own heart   against itself   pin

dreams on you   come light   have

a blast   in that   chthonic place

we swim   in light   angels

dancing on   a pin   of sound

Stopping on Delos

I climb a hill
to the temple
of Isis.

Her missing face
looks out
to sea.

All her dreams
are nautical.

Poppies enfold
her granite
pedestal.

A bump, a burr,
a barnacle,

flecked with red
paint, clings to
her waist.

Stub-thumb
of an ancient
child. Pagan

mother, take
my hand—tiny,
unsculpted, living.

NOTES

The serpent of "Incantation" has origins in the Sumerian creation story
of Inanna:
". . . The tree grew thick,
But its bark did not split.
Then a serpent who could not be charmed
Made its nest in the roots of the *huluppu*-tree.
The *Anzu*-bird set his young in the branches of the tree.
And the dark maid Lilith built her home in the trunk."
—"The *Huluppu*-Tree," from *Inanna, Queen of Heaven and Earth*,
translated by Diane Wolkstein and Samuel Noah Kramer.

A Sumerian belief worth noting here is that the universe was engendered
from, and surrounded by, water. From within, the world appeared to be a
round lake.

The title "Poem for Jesus's Son" was suggested by the Velvet
Underground song, "Heroin," as well as by Denis Johnson's stories.

"Dreamway" was a nickname coined in the 1940s for the Pennsylvania
Turnpike. Some phrases in the poem are taken from Ginger Strand's
nonfiction book, *Killer on the Road*, about violence and the American
Interstate.

Gravity and Grace is the title of a philosophical work by Simone Weil.

The poem "Your Last Drive" was suggested by Thomas Hardy's poem of
the same title.

The title "Lady with an Ermine" is taken from da Vinci's painting.

"Letter to a Gowanus Novice" owes debts to John Donne's *Holy Sonnets* and Brenda Shaughnessy's "Letter to a Crevice Novice."

Some phrases in "On the Origins of Language" are taken from a lecture given by Richard Leakey, the paleoanthropologist, at the Turkana Basin Institute in Kenya in 2012.

The poem "Anemone" was suggested by JMW Turner's painting, "Peace—Burial at Sea."

The title "Song Traversing a Tenebrous World" is taken from a painting by the San Francisco-based painter, Tino Rodriguez.

The title "Girl with Doves" is taken from the Greek stele housed at the Metropolitan Museum of Art.

Some phrases in "Crook and Cradle" are taken from an advertisement for Body Armor.

The closing image of "Falassarna" was suggested by H.D., who wrote: "I know, I feel / the meanings that words hide; // they are anagrams, cryptograms, / little boxes, conditioned / to hatch butterflies."
	—*The Walls Do Not Fall*

The title "Mothlight" is taken from Stan Brakhage's film.

A "thin place" is a pagan Celtic term, later adopted by Christians, for a mesmerizing place or state of being in which one feels close to the divine.

Acknowledgments

The author wishes to thank the editors of the following publications in which these poems, sometimes in different forms, appeared.

The Brooklyn Quarterly, *The Hopkins Review*, *The New Criterion*, *The New Republic*, *The Paris Review*, *Parnassus*, *Poetry Daily*, *Psychology Tomorrow*, *Small Spiral Notebook*, and *The Southampton Review*.

These poems were written with the help and encouragement of too many to name. Special thanks to my first poetry teacher, Marie Howe; and to Lucie Brock-Broido; Henri Cole; Billy Collins; Linda Gregg; Richard Howard; Marie Ponsot; Alice Quinn and Jean Valentine. Deep gratitude to family, friends, and editors for their continued faith, inspiration, and readership; especially Stephen Byler; Jane Carr; Ben Downing; Laura Dunn; Sacha Evans; David Gates; Jared Hayley; Chloe Honum; David Kaplan; Rachel King; Paul La Farge; Herbert Leibowitz; Kelly Loudenberg; Margot Lurie; Ricardo Maldonado; Ryan Murphy; Jeremy Pataky; Michael Romanos; Wendy Salinger; Bernard Schwartz; Erika Seidman; Brenda Shaughnessy; Julie Sheehan; Jesse Sheidlower; Laura Sillerman; Amanda Turner; Jonathan Wells; Joel Whitney and David Yezzi. Thanks to the Jerome Foundation, MacDowell Colony, Virginia Center for the Creative Arts, New York State Summer Writers Institute, 92Y Unterberg Poetry Center, Aegean Centre, and Pierrepont School for their support. Special thanks to Martha Rhodes.

Grace Bonner is a former director of the 92Y Poetry Center and a mentor in PEN's prison writing program. She has taught literature and creative writing at the Pierrepont School in Westport, Connecticut, and in Paros, Greece. She has written a memoir, *Ghost Tracks*, and lives in Montana and upstate New York.

Publication of this book was made possible by grants and donations. We are also grateful to those individuals who participated in our 2015 Build a Book Program. They are:

Jan Bender-Zanoni, Betsy Bonner, Deirdre Brill, Carla & Stephen Carlson, Liza Charlesworth, Catherine Degraw & Michael Connor, Greg Egan, Martha Webster & Robert Fuentes, Anthony Guetti, Hermann Hesse, Deming Holleran, Joy Jones, Katie Childs & Josh Kalscheur, Michelle King, David Lee, Howard Levy, Jillian Lewis, Juliana Lewis, Owen Lewis, Alice St. Claire Long & David Long, Catherine McArthur, Nathan McClain, Carolyn Murdoch, Tracey Orick, Kathleen Ossip, Eileen Pollack, Barbara Preminger, Vinode Ramgopal, Roni Schotter, Soraya Shalforoosh, Marjorie & Lew Tesser, David Tze, Abby Wender, and Leah Nanako Winkler.